ALL ABOUT FOOD

DAIRY FOODS & DRINKS

Cecilia Fitzsimons

Silver Burdett Press
Parsippany, New Jersey

First American publication
1997 by Silver Burdett Press
A Division of Simon & Schuster
299 Jefferson Road,
Parsippany, NJ 07054-0480

A ZOË BOOK

Original text © 1997 Cecilia Fitzsimons
© 1997 Zoë Books Limited

Devised and produced by
Zoë Books Limited
15 Worthy Lane
Winchester
Hampshire SO23 7AB
England

First published in Great Britain in 1997 by
Zoë Books Limited
15 Worthy Lane
Winchester
Hampshire SO23 7AB

Printed in Belgium by Proost N.V.
Editors: Kath Davies, Imogen Dawson
Design & production: Sterling Associates
Illustrations: Cecilia Fitzsimons

ISBN 0-382-39595-6 (LSB) 10 9 8 7 6 5 4 3 2 1
ISBN 0-382-39600-6 (PBK) 10 9 8 7 6 5 4 3 2 1

Cataloging-in-Publication Data

Fitzsimons, Cecilia
Dairy Foods & drinks/by Cecilia Fitzsimons.
    p. cm.—(All about food)
Originally published: Winchester, Hampshire, England: Zoë Books, 1996.
Includes bibliographical references and index.
    Summary: Explains the history and use of dairy products and
such drinks as coffee, tea, and soft drinks. Includes related recipes.
    1. Cookery (Dairy Products)—Juvenile literature. 2. Beverages—
Juvenile Literature. 3. Dairy Products—Juvenile Literature.
4. Nuts—Juvenile Literature. 5. Spices—Juvenile Literature.
[1. Dairy products. 2. Beverages. 3. Cookery—Dairy products.]
I. Title. II. Series.
TX759.F57 1997   95-31939
641.3'7—dc 20   CIP
                                     AC

Contents

Introduction

Dairy foods are made from milk. They include cream, butter, cheese, and yogurt. A dairy used to be the clean, cool room on a farm where these foods were made. Today a dairy is also a type of factory.

dairymaid

cave painting

Thousands of years ago people hunted wild animals and gathered fruits and berries for food. They began to tame horses and reindeer, and they may have drunk the animals' milk. These **Stone Age** people also collected eggs to eat as they wandered from place to place.

When people began to settle and to grow crops, they tamed, or **domesticated**, wild animals such as sheep and goats. Cattle were the last animals to be tamed, about 8,000 years ago. Wild cows can be very fierce!

Water is the natural drink for all animals. Until about 150 years ago, water in towns was often infected with disease. Everybody drank beer, wine, or milk instead. Water must be boiled to kill any **germs** that it contains.

People discovered that **herbs** could be added to hot water to make a flavored tea, or **tisane**. Some drinks were bitter, so they were sweetened with honey or sugar.

Today in **developed** countries water is piped into our homes. It is cleansed, or **purified**, before it reaches us. Dirty waste water is removed in pipes called **sewers**.

In the kitchen

You will find easy-to-follow recipes for different foods and drinks in this book. Here are some points to remember when you prepare food:

1. Sharp knives, hot liquids, and pans are dangerous. *Always ask an adult* to help you when you are preparing or cooking food in the kitchen.

2. Before you start, put on an apron and wash your hands.

3. All the ingredients and equipment are listed at the beginning of each recipe. Make sure that you have everything you need before you start.

4. Read the instructions. Measure or weigh the ingredients very carefully.

Think green

We often throw away things that we could use again, or **recycle**. If we reused some of our newspapers, cans, bottles, and plastic packaging, we would help to improve our **environment**.

Dairy products and drinks are sold in metal, glass, plastic, or paper packaging. In this book you will find some ideas for using dairy products, drinks, and their packages.

Milk

Milk is produced only by female **mammals**. All newborn mammals, including human beings, feed on milk from their mother's body. The milk is made in a part of the mother's body called a **mammary gland**. The young mammals suck the milk from the mother's breasts or udders through a teat.

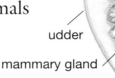
a cow's udder

udder

mammary gland

duct

teat

Cows' milk is most often used to drink and to make dairy products. Milk also comes from goats, sheep, buffalo, and other animals. Cows that graze on rich, green fields produce the best quality milk. These grasses grow in areas such as The Great Plains in the United States, Devon in England, Normandy in France, Argentina, New Zealand, and southern Australia.

Some people cannot drink milk. Their bodies cannot **digest** the milk sugar, or lactose. Most people, especially in the United States and northern European countries, do drink milk.

About 500 years ago, European explorers traveled to the Americas, to Africa, and later to Australia and New Zealand. They survived these long journeys because they usually took cows or goats with them. The animals' milk often saved the travelers from starving.

Food facts

Milk contains **minerals** such as calcium that are necessary for healthy bones and teeth. It also contains **vitamins**, which bodies need to stay healthy. The **protein** in milk is an important food that bodies need to grow.

Soy milk is made from soybeans. People who cannot drink cows' milk can usually drink soy milk instead.

Milk that contains the most fat comes from guinea pigs!

Make a vase

You will need:

a large plastic milk bottle
glue
pasta shapes and dried **pulses**
paints and paintbrushes
clear varnish
scissors

1. *Ask an adult to help you* to cut the top off the bottle.

2. Glue the pasta shapes and pulses onto the bottle. Leave to dry.

3. Paint them and leave them to dry.

4. Paint them with varnish. Leave to dry.

5. Use the vase to hold cut flowers, pencils, paintbrushes, and so on.

Cattle

Domestic cattle are descended from the European wild ox, or auroch. These animals were hunted for their meat and their skins. The auroch had wide, curved horns. They became **extinct** about 350 years ago.

The types, or **breeds**, of cattle we see today are kept for their meat (beef cattle) or their milk (dairy cattle).

auroch

Ayrshire

Brown, white, or red Ayrshire cows come from Scotland.

Holstein-Friesian

Holstein-Friesians are the most popular dairy cows in North America, Britain, and Australia. This breed came originally from the Netherlands.

Guernsey

Jersey

Brown Swiss

Jersey and Guernsey cows come from the Channel Islands. They produce very rich, creamy milk.

Brown Swiss cows come from Switzerland. They are a very strong and healthy breed.

A cow produces milk only after she has given birth to a calf. Dairy cows usually have one calf every year. The calf stays with its mother and feeds on her milk for four days. Then it is raised with other calves. The cow is milked twice a day and will produce milk for up to 10 months.

a Holstein-Friesian cow and calf

Play "Spot the cow"

You will need:

a scrapbook

scissors

glue or transparent tape

pictures, postcards, and photographs of cattle.

1. Collect pictures of as many different breeds of cattle as possible.

2. Divide your pictures into sets of different breeds (e.g., Ayrshires, Jerseys).

3. Glue, or tape the pictures into your scrapbook.

4. Take your scrapbook with you when you go into the countryside.

5. Put a check mark by each breed you see. How many breeds did you see? Which breed is the most common?

Think green

In parts of the United States and Britain, milk is sold in glass bottles. The bottles are returned and recycled. This is the most environmentally friendly way to buy milk.

9

Milk from other animals

ibex

Goats and sheep are kept for milk in hot, dry Mediterranean and African countries. Their milk is used to make cheese and yogurt.

Goats

Saanen

Domestic goats are descended from the wild mountain ibex. The wild ancestor of sheep was the mouflon. Both these mountain animals lived in the Middle East. People hunted them for food, wool, and milk.

Goats are usually kept on land that is too steep or poor to grow crops. Saanen goats were bred in Switzerland. Anglo-Nubian goats were **crossbred** from Sudan and Indian goats. They are now found all over the world.

Anglo-Nubian

Sheep

Most dairy sheep are found in Europe. Two well-known breeds are Friesian sheep from Holland and Germany and Laucaune sheep from France. The famous Roquefort cheese is made with Laucaune milk.

mouflon

Friesian

Food facts

One goat will produce its own weight in milk every 14 days.

Goats' milk is easy for people to digest.

Most people in Europe drank sheep's milk until about 500 years ago. Then cows' milk became more popular. Cows are easier to milk than sheep, and cows produce more milk per animal.

Other dairy animals

In Lapland, people use reindeer milk, and in the Caucasus Mountains in eastern Europe, they use horses' (mares') milk. In Egypt, India, and the Far East, buffaloes are kept for milk. The yak is the wild cow of the Himalayas. Most yaks are now domesticated. Camels provide milk in the Middle East and in North Africa.

camel

reindeer

horse

yak

buffalo

Think green

Materials such as wool and cotton occur naturally. Other materials, called **synthetics**, are made from all kinds of things, including petroleum. The ways in which synthetics are made can **pollute** our environment.

Look at the labels on the clothes you wear. Are they made from natural or synthetic materials?

Weave a friendship bracelet

You will need:

yarn or heavy cotton thread in three different colors

scissors, transparent tape

a piece of poster paper

1. Cut three pieces of yarn, each 27 in (70 cm) long. Choose three different colors. Knot them together at one end, leaving a 2 in (5 cm) tassel. Tape the knot to the top of the paper.

2. Give each thread a number, 1, 2, and 3. Hold thread 2. Loop and knot thread 1 around it. Push the knot up and tighten.

3. Repeat, so that you have two knots.

4. Hold thread 3 and knot thread 1 around it twice, so that you have two knots on thread 3. (Thread 1 finishes on the right.)

5. Repeat steps 2–4, using thread 2 (now on the left). Two knots go around thread 3, and two knots around thread 1.

6. Continue knotting the left-hand thread until your bracelet is long enough to fit your wrist.

7. To finish, knot all the threads together. Cut off the ends, leaving a 2 in (5 cm) tassel. Place around your wrist and tie the tassels together.

From milking to milkshakes

Cows must be milked twice every day. For thousands of years, people milked cows by hand.

Today cows are usually milked by machines in a large milking room. Their udders are carefully washed, and rubber cups are placed over their teats. The milking machine pumps the milk into a refrigerated storage tank.

Every day a tanker collects the milk and takes it to a dairy.

hand milking

a modern milking room

Cream

Cream floats to the surface of milk. Whole milk has all its cream in it. Part-skim milk has some of its cream. Most of the cream is removed from skim milk. Cream and milk are used in desserts and to make butter, cheese, yogurt, ice cream, sauces, custards, and flavored drinks.

cream

strawberries and cream

cheese

milk

butter

Milk contains **bacteria**, which will soon turn it sour, especially in hot weather. Bacteria may also cause diseases such as tuberculosis.

It is important to be clean, or hygienic, at every stage of milk production. Most milk is heated, or pasteurized, to kill any bacteria in it. Long-life milk is called UHT (ultra high temperature). It will last for up to 6 months.

Canned milk has been heated to kill any bacteria and to reduce the amount of water in it. This process is called sterilization. Canned milk is sold as condensed or evaporated milk.

Milk can be dried by passing it over a hot roller or spraying it through hot air. Dried milk will keep for at least 6 months.

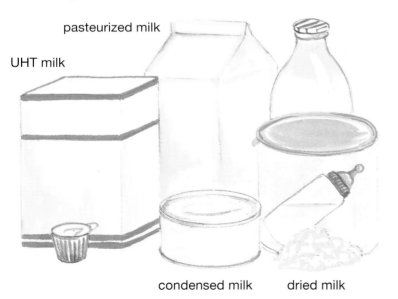

pasteurized milk

UHT milk

condensed milk   dried milk

Food facts

Spinning milk breaks down fat into its small particles. It blends them evenly, so the cream does not rise to the top. This is called homogenized milk.

Make a chocolate milkshake

You will need:

a glass of milk

1 teaspoon of cocoa powder or chocolate syrup

sugar

---

a screw-topped container

some boiled water

a spoon for stirring the mixture

1. *Ask an adult* to help you to heat the water.

2. Put the cocoa into the screw-topped container.

3. *Ask an adult* to help you to add a little hot water to the cocoa. Add a little sugar. Stir well to make a smooth paste.

4. Pour in the milk. Screw the lid on tightly. Shake well until the milk is frothy and the chocolate is all mixed in.

5. Pour into a glass and drink.

Cream, butter, and yogurt

cream

whole milk

Cream is the fatty layer that floats on top of milk. It contains most of the vitamins in milk. Cream can be skimmed from milk by hand or by machine.

There are different types of cream: light cream, heavy – or whipping – cream, and half-and-half, equal parts cream and milk. The fat content of cream varies from about 18 to 40 percent.

Thick clotted cream is made by heating cream slowly. It is made in southwest England and in Asia. Sour cream and *crème fraîche* from France taste tangy. Cream can be canned, frozen, and sold in spray cans.

Butter is cream that has been shaken or churned until the fat separates from the watery buttermilk. Butter will turn bad, or **rancid**, quite quickly unless it is kept in a cool place, such as a refrigerator. Salt can be added to butter to preserve it.

butter pats

butter molds

butter churn

Food facts

In India, ghee is cooking butter that has been heated and strained.

Margarine can be used instead of butter. It is made from vegetable and/or animal oils. A French chemist called Mège-Mouriès invented it in the 1860s.

Butter used to be made in a butter churn. It was shaped with wooden tools (called pats) to make a rectangular block, or butter pat.

Decorated butter pats were pressed in wooden molds.

Yogurt is made from sour milk. People have eaten yogurt since ancient times. It was popular with Egyptian, Greek, and Indian people long before it was well-known in Europe and North America. Today fruit, nuts, and honey may be added to yogurt to give it different flavors.

Ice cream

The Italians began to make ice cream about 500 years ago.

Traditional ice cream is frozen cream, flavored with fruit and vanilla. Today some ice cream is made from dried milk or custard, and some may contain no milk or cream at all.

Think green

Cream, butter, yogurt, margarine, and ice cream are all sold in plastic boxes. How can you reuse the boxes? Try: sandwich boxes, plant containers, paint pots, milkshake shakers, pencil holders, and even CD boxes.

Make your own ice cream

You will need:

½ pt (300 ml) heavy cream
½ pt (300 ml) milk
4 oz (100 g) sugar
vanilla or other flavoring
_____

teaspoon

1. *Ask an adult* to help you to put the milk into a saucepan and warm gently. Add the sugar and stir until it has dissolved. Cool.

2. Whip the cream and stir it gently into the milk.

3. Add 1 teaspoon of vanilla flavoring for vanilla ice cream, 4 teaspoons of cocoa for chocolate ice cream, or 1 lb (500 g) mashed fresh strawberries for strawberry ice cream.

4. Place the mixture in a shallow dish (metal if possible) and put it into the freezer.

5. After 1 hour take it out and whisk or mash it smooth. Refreeze. Repeat this 2 or 3 times until the ice cream is frozen.

Cheese

mozzarella

Camembert

Brie

cottage cheese

The first cheeses were probably eaten thousands of years ago. They may have been made by accident. Milk would soon have turned into cheese if it were kept in a bag made from an animal's stomach.

Milk goes sour and curdles when **enzymes** are added to it. There are enzymes in rennet, which is found in a calf's stomach. Rennet makes milk separate into solid **curds** and liquid **whey**. The curds can be pressed to form a firm cheese.

Cheese is salted, dried, or smoked. Some cheeses are left for several months to produce a strong flavor, or "mature."

Soft cheeses are loose and creamy.

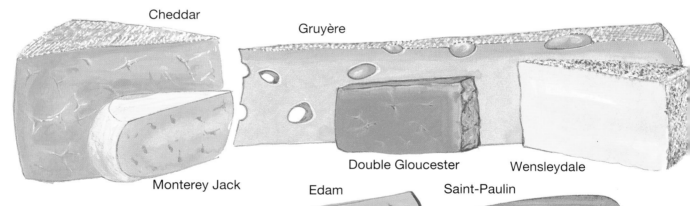

Cheddar

Gruyère

Double Gloucester

Wensleydale

Monterey Jack

Edam

Saint-Paulin

Semihard cheeses are firm. They are pressed and then matured.

Food facts

It takes 20 gallons (77 liters) of milk to make one Stilton cheese.

Cheesecloth is a loose woven cloth. It is used to line a cheese mold.

Hard cheeses are grated and served with pasta. Parmesan and Pecorino (Italy) are hard and dry.

Parmesan

Pecorino

grated Parmesan

Blue cheeses

The blue pattern in some cheeses is a mold. It gives them a strong flavor.

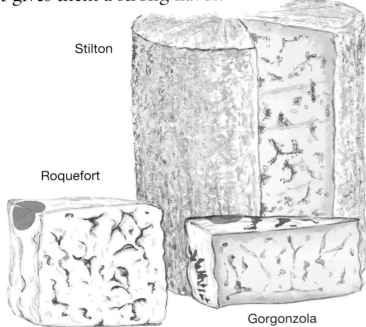

Stilton

Roquefort

Gorgonzola

Gorgonzola (Italy) and Roquefort (France) have been made for at least 1,000 years. Roquefort is a sheep's milk cheese, which matures in underground caves. Stilton was first sold at the Bell Inn, Stilton, England, almost 300 years ago.

Think green

Wooden cheese boxes can be washed and decorated. They make attractive jewelry boxes or boxes for other treasures.

Make a cheese dip

You will need:

5 oz (150 g) semihard cheese

6 oz (170 g) cottage cheese

5 oz (150 g) sour cream

2 tablespoons (30 ml) mayonnaise

serving bowl
wooden bowl

1. Crumble the cheese into small pieces in a bowl.

2. Mix in the other ingredients.

3. Serve with potato chips and vegetable sticks.

Try different flavors by using different cheeses. Blue cheeses will give a strong flavor. Mild Cheddar is more mellow.

Add other flavors such as chopped onion, celery, ham, garlic, poppy seeds, or curry powder.

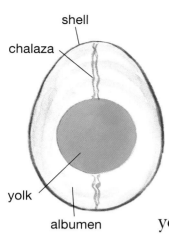

shell
chalaza
yolk
albumen

Eggs

Eggs provide people with protein. Today we mostly eat chickens' eggs, but people also enjoy duck, geese, quail, guinea fowl, pigeon and ostrich eggs.

An egg has a hard outer shell made of calcium. The shell contains the egg white, or albumen, which surrounds the yellow yolk. The "stringy bit" that holds the yolk in place is called the chalaza.

Domestic chickens are descended from Red Jungle fowl that still live in the forests of India. About 4,000 years ago they were kept for cock fighting. Chickens spread to Europe and China, and about 500 years ago they were taken by Columbus to the Americas.

There are many breeds of chickens. The Dorking may have been brought to Britain by the Romans. The Leghorn originally came from Italy, while New Hampshire and Rhode Island Red are North American breeds. Crossbred chickens are now the most common egg layers. Each bird may lay up to 300 eggs a year.

duck
chicken
quail

Dorking
Leghorn

Red Jungle fowl

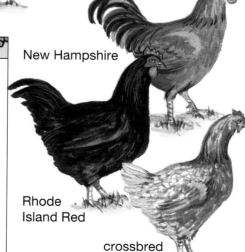

New Hampshire

Rhode Island Red

crossbred

Think green

Find out where the eggs come from before you eat them.

Marine turtles are an **endangered species**. Turtle eggs must not be taken from their nests.

Many chickens are raised by intensive farming methods. One chicken house may hold up to 50,000 birds. Free-range chickens live in more natural conditions. They can move around inside and outside their shelters.

Duck and goose eggs are larger, richer, and more oily in taste than hens' eggs. Aylesbury ducks and other farm ducks are descended from wild mallard ducks. The Muscovy duck from South America may be more closely related to geese.

Farm geese are descended from wild graylag geese. Toulouse geese come from France.

Pilgrim geese were taken to North America by people known as "pilgrims," who left Europe about 370 years ago to live in the New World.

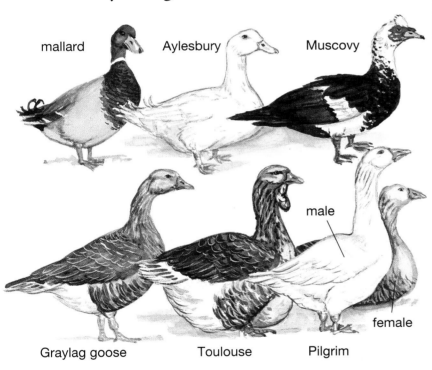

mallard   Aylesbury   Muscovy

male

female

Graylag goose   Toulouse   Pilgrim

Food facts

Eggs contain protein, fat, minerals such as calcium and iron and Vitamins A, B, D, and E.

Eggs are connected with Easter and other religious or springtime festivals. The egg is a sign, or symbol, of new life.

Decorated eggs

You will need:

fresh eggs (not chilled)

food coloring

a soft-lead pencil

scraps of colored paper
  or material

a saucepan

a large spoon

1. Choose one egg for each person in your family, or your friends. Draw a funny picture of each person's face on the eggs.

2. Make paper or cloth hats for the eggs.

3. Put enough water in the saucepan to cover the eggs. Add a few drops of coloring.

4. *Ask an adult* to boil the water. Put each egg on the spoon and slowly lower it into the water.

5. Cook the eggs 6-8 minutes.

6. Put the eggs into eggcups (or large plastic bottle caps). Put on their hats. Serve with bread and butter.

Chocolate drinks

Chocolate comes from beans that grow on the trunk of the cacao tree in South America. The drink called *xocoatl* was served to the Spanish explorers by the Aztec people more than 400 years ago in what is now Mexico. Today cacao trees are grown in Central and South America, Sri Lanka, Madagascar, and West Africa.

Cacao beans are removed from the pod and are **fermented**. Only after they have turned reddish brown, do the beans develop their chocolate flavor. Then the beans are dried and ground into a paste, which is hardened to form bitter cooking chocolate. The chocolate is dried and ground to make cocoa powder.

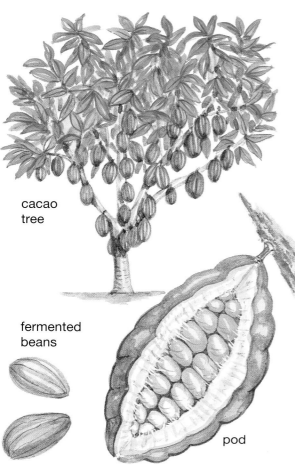

cacao tree

fermented beans

pod

About 400 years ago dark chocolate became a popular, but very expensive, drink in Europe. Chocolate houses were the fashionable places to meet. The first eating chocolate was made in Britain by Fry and Sons in 1847. Milk chocolate was created in Switzerland in 1876.

Food facts

Chocolate is rich in fats, proteins, minerals, **carbohydrates**, and vitamins A and D.

Carob, or locust bean, is used instead of chocolate in some recipes. This bean is from the locust tree, which comes from the Mediterranean.

Today chocolate is used in many drinks, such as cocoa, milkshakes, and hot chocolate. It is used in a wide variety of candies, cakes, desserts, and cookies. Some South American savory dishes are also flavored with chocolate.

Make a hot chocolate drink

You will need:

1 cup of milk

2 teaspoons of cocoa powder

1 or 2 teaspoons of sugar

1. Put the cocoa and sugar into a cup.

2. Mix in a little cold milk until you have a smooth paste.

3. Pour the rest of the milk into a saucepan.

4. *Ask an adult* to help you to heat the milk slowly until it is hot, but not boiling.

5. *Ask an adult* to help you to pour the hot milk into the cup carefully. Mix well and drink when it has cooled a little.

Think green

Reuse or recycle chocolate boxes and wrappings. Chocolate boxes can make attractive storage boxes. Bright colored chocolate wrapping paper can be used to make pictures or to decorate storage boxes.

Coffee

Coffee is a drink made by soaking, or **infusing**, roasted, ground coffee beans in hot water. There are many different ways of infusing coffee.

Coffee beans grow on an evergreen shrub that originally grew in Ethiopia. Each bright red coffee berry contains two seeds, the coffee beans. The beans do not ripen at the same time, so the best quality coffee is picked by hand.

Coffee beans are dried in the sun and then roasted. They turn brown and the coffee flavor develops.

flowers

beans

coffee berries

Coffee contains caffeine, which can make some people feel "jumpy," or keep them awake. Legends tell of a goatherd who lived about 1,000 years ago. His goats began to dance after they had eaten coffee berries! Arab people first used coffee as a medicine.

Coffee houses opened in the city of Mecca, in Arabia, in the **Middle Ages**. They spread to Europe, where the first ones opened in Italy in 1580, in England in 1650, and in North America in 1668. They were later called cafés, which is the French word for coffee.

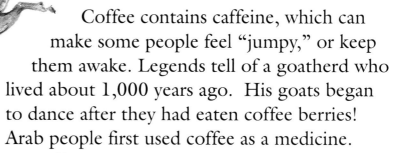

Think green
Reuse coffee jars. Keep dried herbs or nuts in small, clean jars and pasta or cereals in larger jars. Make decorated labels for the jars.

Coffee is now grown in Central and South America, the Caribbean, Africa, and Asia. There are many different varieties of coffee plants. Different beans are mixed in blends such as Kenyan, Costa Rican, Colombian, and Mocha. Roasting changes the coffee flavor. Beans are dark roast, medium, or light.

dark roast

medium roast

light roast

ground coffee

instant coffee

Instant coffee was first produced about 60 years ago. Strong, liquid coffee is dried by spraying it through hot air and by freeze or vacuum drying. Then the powder can be dissolved in hot water to make liquid coffee again.

Food facts

The caffeine in coffee can be removed by steaming and washing. This is called "decaffeinated" coffee.

It takes about 4,000 berries to make 2¼ lb (1 kg) of coffee.

Ground, dried dandelion or chicory roots are sometimes added to coffee for flavor.

Make iced coffee

You will need:

½-1 teaspoon of instant coffee

2 teaspoons of sugar (if liked)

½ teaspoon of cocoa powder

½ cup milk

½ cup crushed ice cubes

spray can of whipped cream

a large, screw-topped jar

a tall glass

1. *Ask an adult* to help you to warm the milk in a saucepan.

2. Add the coffee. Stir until it is dissolved. Leave until cold.

3. Put the ice into the jar. Pour in the coffee.

4. Screw on the lid tightly and shake well.

5. Taste. Add more cold milk if too strong a taste. Pour into a glass.

6. Spray the whipped cream on top and serve sprinkled with cocoa powder.

Try adding other ingredients such as vanilla or chocolate ice cream, grated orange peel, or nuts.

Tea

Tea is an infusion of leaves in hot water. It is served with lemon or milk.

Fresh tea leaves are dark green and glossy. They grow on an evergreen bush that is related to the camellia. Tea plants have white or pink flowers.

Tea plants were grown in China around 5,000 years ago. Tea is now grown in India, China, Japan, Sri Lanka, Southeast Asia, and Africa.

There are many varieties and blends of tea, such as Assam, China, Ceylon, Darjeeling, Earl Grey, Jasmine, and Lapsang Souchong.

Loose tea leaves are sold in packets or put into tea bags. Instant tea, like coffee, is dried liquid tea.

tea

two tea leaves and a bud

instant tea

tea bags

loose tea

Tea leaves are carefully picked by hand. For the best tea, only the top two leaves and the bud of each stalk are taken.

Green tea leaves are heated and rolled several times until the leaves turn dark green.

Black tea leaves have been dried until they wither. They are then rolled and left to ferment. When they are dried, they are black and crisp.

Think green

Use loose tea rather than tea bags to save paper.

Put used tea leaves around the roots of rose and camellia bushes. This feeds the plants and helps to keep the soil moist.

24

Herb teas

An herb tea is called a tisane. Boiling water is poured onto fresh or dried herbs, and the mixture is left to stand. Sometimes the drink is sweetened with honey.

Food facts

Tea contains caffeine, which can keep you awake, and an acid called tannin, which can make it taste bitter.

About 150 years ago sailing ships called "clipper ships" raced from China to Britain to be the first home with the new year's cargo of tea.

A tax on tea helped to start the American Revolution. The people said that they would have "no taxation without representation" in the British Parliament. In 1773 they protested by throwing the tea cargo into the harbor at Boston, Massachusetts.

Make a cup of tea

You will need:

water

tea

milk *or* lemon

sugar

___

a knife

a teapot

a teaspoon

mugs or teacups

1. *Ask an adult* to help you to slice the lemon.

2. *Ask an adult* to boil some water in a kettle.

3. Warm the teapot with a little warm water. Pour out the water.

4. Put one teaspoon of tea for each person and "one for the pot" into the teapot.

5. *Ask an adult* to pour the boiling water into the teapot.

6. Leave the tea to "brew" for 2-4 minutes.

7. Pour the tea. Add milk and sugar, if you wish, or slices of lemon.

Soft drinks

"Soft" drinks are usually made from water mixed with natural or artificial flavors. The water can be naturally still or bubbly. Some still water has had a gas added to it to make it sparkling. This water is called "carbonated."

Soft drinks are also made from fruit juices or other parts of plants. The flavors come from crushed plant roots, leaves, and seeds.

soft drinks

a natural spring

Mineral waters

Some rocks are full of tiny holes, like sponges. They are called porous rocks. As water passes through the rock to the surface, it may become bubbly. It may also take up minerals and their flavors from the rocks. Mineral waters are bottled and sold.

Mineral waters have been drunk as medicines for thousands of years. Famous towns such as Bath in England and Vichy in France grew up around mineral springs. People traveled great distances to drink these waters.

Food facts

Water from different springs contains different minerals. Look at the labels on bottles of mineral water to see where they come from and which minerals they contain.

Kola nuts contain the chemicals caffeine and tannin. Some cola drinks are decaffeinated.

Still lemonade was on sale in Paris in 1676. Carbonated water was developed about 200 years ago.

Cola

The flavor in bubbly cola drinks comes from kola nuts. These are the seeds of an evergreen African tree. Kola trees are grown in many **tropical** countries. Their flowers are yellow, and they produce star-shaped fruit.

Cola drinks were first sold as a health tonic in Atlanta, Georgia, in 1886.

cola

kola nuts

Think green

Recycle cans and plastic and glass bottles. Drinks cans are made of a metal called aluminium. It is mined in tropical rain forests. Trees are cut down, and the land and air are being polluted. If you recycle your cans, you will help to save the rain forests.

How many things can you make from lemonade bottles? Here are some ideas:

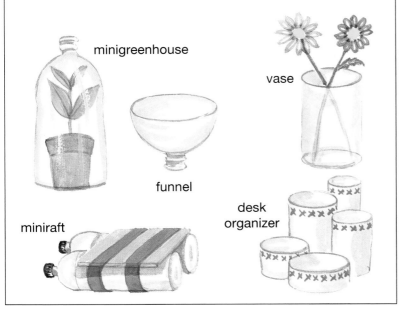

minigreenhouse

vase

funnel

desk organizer

miniraft

Make old-fashioned lemonade

You will need:

3 lemons

3-4 tablespoons of sugar

1 quart (or 1 liter) boiling water

heat resistant container

strainer

1. Wash the lemons. *Ask an adult* to help you to cut the lemons. Slice half of one lemon and cut the others into small pieces.

2. Put the lemon pieces and their juice into a large, heat-resistant container.

3. Add the sugar.

4. *Ask an adult* to help you to boil the water and pour it carefully into the container.

5. Stir well and leave for 30 minutes.

6. Pour the mixture carefully through a strainer into a clean container.

7. Chill. Serve with ice, slices of lemon, and sprigs of mint.

Honey and sugar

honeybee

Sugar sweetens food and drinks. It occurs naturally in fruit, honey, sugar cane, and some root vegetables.

Honeybees collect **nectar** from flowers and store it in the wax honeycomb in their hives. Our hunter-gatherer ancestors collected wild honey, and ancient peoples such as the Egyptians kept bees. More than 500 years ago, monks and nuns made a drink called mead from honey. Wax from their beehives was used to make church candles.

a wild bee's honeycomb

beehive

Sugar cane

sugar cane

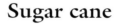

Sugar cane is a giant, tropical grass that grows up to 24 feet (7 meters) tall. Its stems are cut and crushed to produce sugar syrup.

Sugar cane originally grew on South Pacific islands. Arab traders first took sugar to Europe, and about 500 years ago, Venetian merchants could **refine** sugar to make it fine and white. Today sugar cane is grown in North and South America, the Caribbean, Asia, and Australia.

Sugar beet

The sugar beet is a white beetroot, which contains sugar. It grows in cool climates, especially in northern Europe.

sugar beet

Food facts

Sugar cane needs 80-90 inches (200-230 cm) of rain a year to produce a good crop.

Sugar provides our bodies with extra energy quickly.

Sugar is bad for your teeth. It causes acid to form, which attacks your teeth.

28

Maple syrup is the sap of the North American sugar maple tree. It is usually eaten with pancakes for breakfast or with desserts.

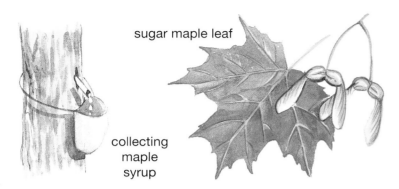

sugar maple leaf

collecting maple syrup

Molasses is a thick, dark brown sugar syrup. Golden syrup and white sugar are made from refined molasses. Brown sugars are unrefined.

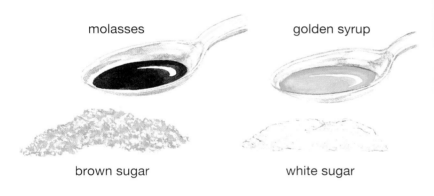

molasses

golden syrup

brown sugar

white sugar

Think green

In some areas, such as Mauritius, the tropical rain forest is being destroyed to make way for huge sugar plantations.

Cane toads from South America were taken to Australia to eat beetles that attacked sugar cane. These toads eat many other things and are now destroying native Australian animals.

Find out where the sugar you use comes from.

Make peppermint creams

You will need:
1 egg white

1 lb (450 g) confectioners' sugar

3 fl oz (75 ml) evaporated milk

few drops of peppermint flavoring

mixing bowl

wooden spoon

baking tray

1. Sift the confectioners' sugar into a bowl.

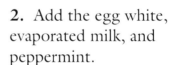

2. Add the egg white, evaporated milk, and peppermint.

3. Mix well into a stiff paste.

4. Dust your hands with some of the sugar. Then take small pieces of paste, roll them into balls, and flatten them slightly.

5. Put them on a baking tray dusted with the sugar and let them dry for about 12 hours.

Glossary

bacteria: tiny organisms that occur in air, water, animals, and plants. They can cause disease and can make food go bad.

breeds: different kinds of the same animal, e.g., Jersey or Ayrshire cattle.

carbohydrates: food substances that are energy rich, such as sugar.

crossbred: plants or animals that grow from different breeds of "parent."

curds: the milk solids that are separated out and made into cheese.

developed: usually refers to Western, industrialized countries, e.g., the United States, France; also includes Japan, Australia.

digest: to change food into a usable form.

domesticate: to tame.

duct: a tube or pipe.

endangered species: a type of animal that is in danger of becoming extinct.

environment: everything around us, such as air, water, and land.

enzyme: proteins that help the body to process, or digest, food.

extinct: a type of animal or plant that has died out.

ferment: cause a chemical change in a substance with yeast or bacteria.

germs: tiny organisms that cause disease.

herbs: plants that do not have woody stems that are used in cooking or to make medicines.

infuse: to soak herbs in liquid so that it takes on their flavor.

mammals: animals whose young feed on milk from their mother's body.

mammary gland: the part of a female mammal's body where milk is made.

Middle Ages: the period of time between about A.D. 500 and 1500. Also called "medieval" times.

minerals: substances in foods that our bodies need to stay healthy.

nectar:	a sweet substance in flowers that bees collect to make honey.
pollute:	to poison air, water, or land.
protein:	an important food substance that people and animals need to live and grow.
pulses:	seeds from pea-like plants that produce fruits in a pod.
purified:	cleansed.
rancid:	bad or spoiled.
recycle:	to make something new out of something that has already been used.
refine:	to purify, or clarify, often by heating.
sewers:	underground pipes that carry away waste materials.
Stone Age:	the time, more than 5,000 years ago, when people used stone, wood, and bones to make tools and weapons. They had not yet learned how to use metals such as bronze and iron.
synthetic:	a substance or material that is made by people and is not produced naturally.
tisanes:	drinks that are flavored with herbs.
tropical:	from the lands near the equator, where the heat from the Sun is strongest. We draw lines on maps to show the position of the tropics and the equator.
vitamins:	the small amounts of different substances in foods that people and animals need for good health.
whey:	the thin, watery liquid milk that is left after the solid curds have separated out.

Further reading

With the Aztecs by Imogen Dawson (Food and Feasts series). New Discovery Books, 1995. This introduction to the ancient Aztec civilization examines the food the people ate, their customs, feasts, and festivals and includes authentic, delicious recipes.

Eat Well by Miriam Moss. Crestwood House 1993. Young readers will learn how to plan a diet to help them stay healthy and will get practical advice that can help improve their confidence and well-being.

Fruit by Cecilia Fitzsimons. (All about Food series). Silver Burdett Press 1996. This book has practical information about various kinds of fruits, taste-tempting recipes, and fascinating projects.

Index of dairy foods and drinks